JOHN LESLEY

Africa

REDBACK publishing

Africa's Economy p.16

Redback Publishing
Suite 6, 13a Narabang Way,
Belrose NSW 2085
Australia

www.redbackpublishing.com
orders@redbackpublishing.com

ISBN 978-1-761400-94-0

Author: John Lesley
Editor: Caroline Thomas
Designer: Redback Publishing

Original illustrations © Redback Publishing 2025

Originated by Redback Publishing

Acknowledgements
Abbreviations: l—left, r—right, b—bottom, t—top, c—centre, m—middle

We would like to thank the following for permission to reproduce photographs (images © Shutterstock unless otherwise stated): p3bl, p11tc golden mask of Egyptian pharaoh, leoks, p7tr USGS, Public domain, via Wikimedia Commons, p7br, p27br Ocean-birth_hg.png: Hannes Grobe, Alfred Wegener Institute for Polar and Marine Research, CC BY-SA 2.5 (https://creativecommons.org/licenses/by-sa/2.5), via Wikimedia Commons, p9br Congo Canyon, Mikenorton, CC BY-SA 3.0 (https://creativecommons.org/licenses/by-sa/3.0), via Wikimedia Commons, p11br farmer in Mardin, Turkey, p12bl Sango-Ijoko Road, Nigeria, Agbebiyi Adekunle Sunday, p12bc Lalibela, Ethiopia, Matyas Rehak, p12br Cairo, Egypt, leshiy985, p17tl Farmer on donkey, Marcos Casiano, p18ml masai women, Aleksandar Todorovic, p19br classroom in Bafoussam, Cameroon, davide bonaldo, p25bc Timbuktu, Mali, DemarK, p31bl kampala-uganda, MehmetO

NATIONAL LIBRARY OF AUSTRALIA
A catalogue record for this book is available from the National Library of Australia

Contents

Africa's People p.18

Unique Heritage p.10

Wildlife in Africa p.28

Earth's 7 Continents

What is a continent?

Continents are very large landmasses that are separated from each other on Earth. Some continents are separated by oceans, but others have land borders with neighbouring continents.

How many continents are there on Earth?

There are seven continents

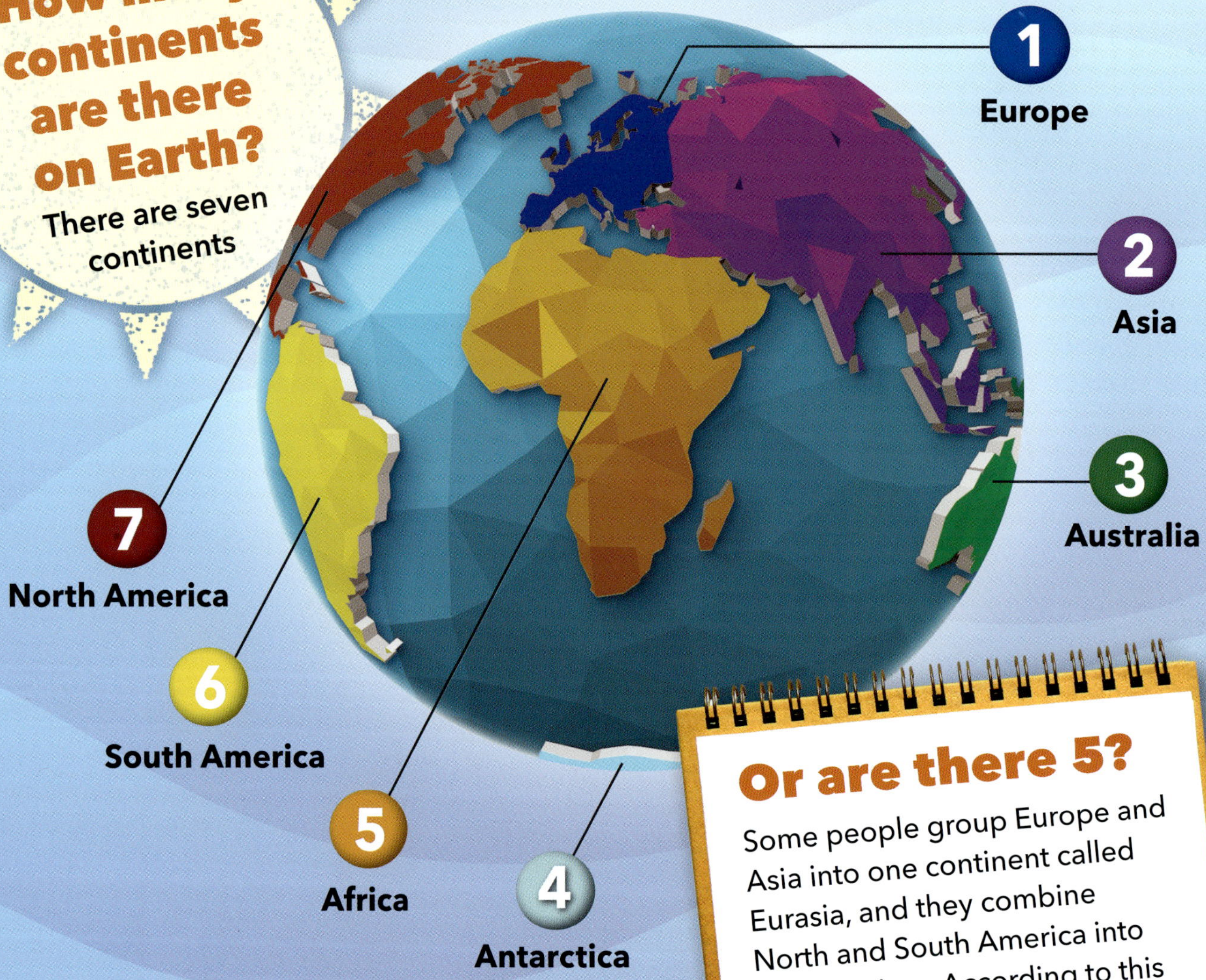

Or are there 5?

Some people group Europe and Asia into one continent called Eurasia, and they combine North and South America into the Americas. According to this method of counting, there are five continents instead of seven.

Origin of Africa

How did the continents form?

The surface of our planet is constantly moving in a very slow process known as plate tectonics. The plates are gigantic slabs of rock that form the surface of our Earth. These plates rest on magma that is hotter and more liquid as it gets deeper towards the Earth's centre. As the heat rises out towards the surface of the Earth, it causes the plates to move around.

Heat moves from the centre to the surface

Plates pull apart *Plates push together*

When these plates move, their edges can either pull apart or push together. Where the plates pull apart, oceans can flow between the landmasses, and where they push together, mountain ranges can form. This process explains how continents form over very long periods of time.

Pangaea and Gondwana

The continents have not always been in the same position as they are today. Millions of years ago, there used to exist a huge mass of land called Pangaea. As tectonic movement caused the sea floor to spread, this supercontinent split apart into two continents called Laurasia and Gondwana.

Laurasia continued to break apart, allowing oceans to flow between the plates that would become Asia, Europe and North America. Gondwana slowly broke apart too, becoming Africa, Antarctica, Australia, South America and the Indian Subcontinent.

The Continent of Africa

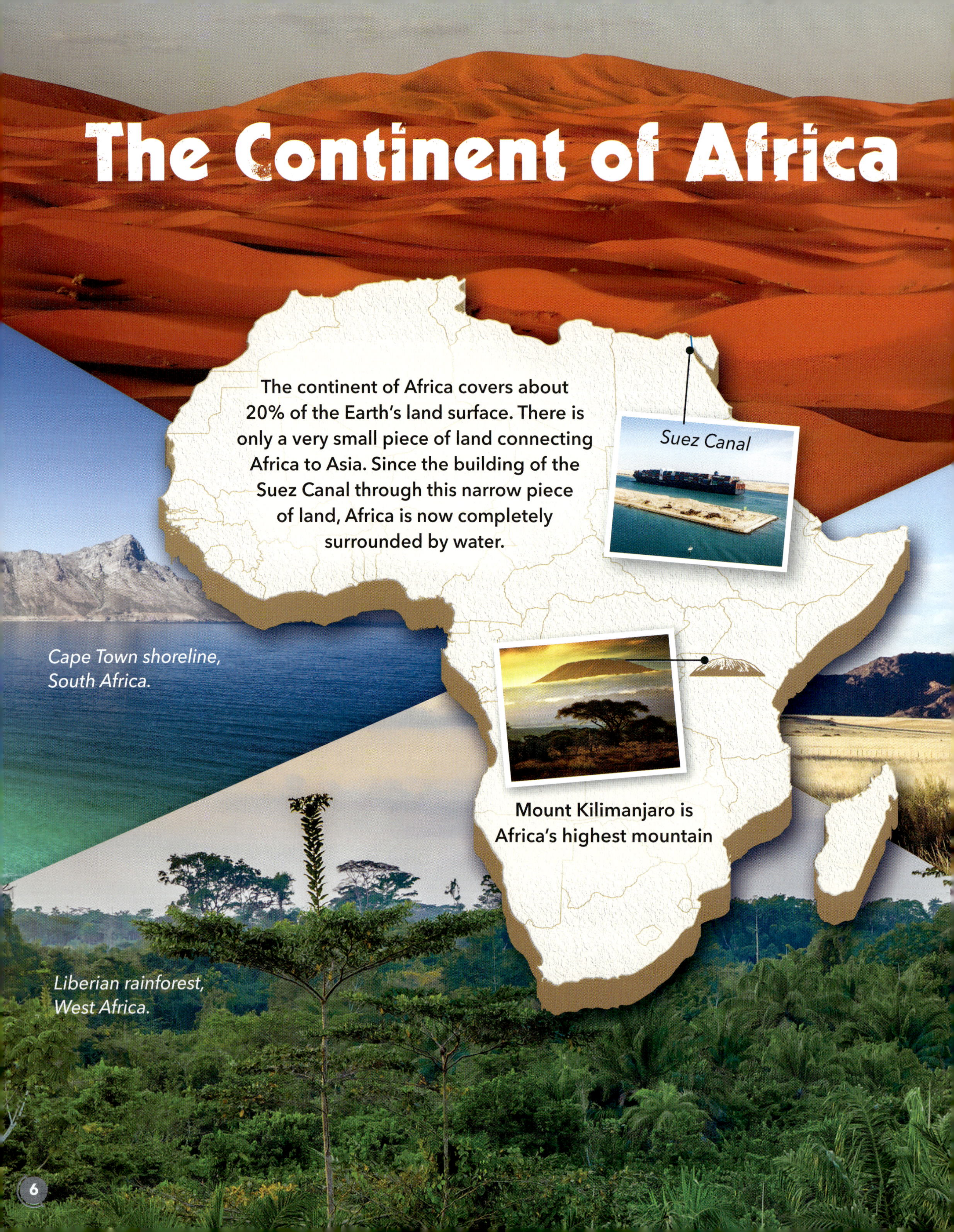

The continent of Africa covers about 20% of the Earth's land surface. There is only a very small piece of land connecting Africa to Asia. Since the building of the Suez Canal through this narrow piece of land, Africa is now completely surrounded by water.

Suez Canal

Mount Kilimanjaro is Africa's highest mountain

Cape Town shoreline, South Africa.

Liberian rainforest, West Africa.

The Sahara Desert, Erg Chebbi, Morocco.

Africa has wide, hot deserts in its north. Moving south, there are grasslands, tropical rainforests and then temperate regions at the far, southern tip.

Savannah grassland in Namibia, southern Africa.

East African Rift

Although Africa is now one single continent, there is a rift running through it that will one day tear it apart into two separate landmasses. This will occur millions of years in the future, as the tectonic forces in the Earth's crust pull Africa apart.

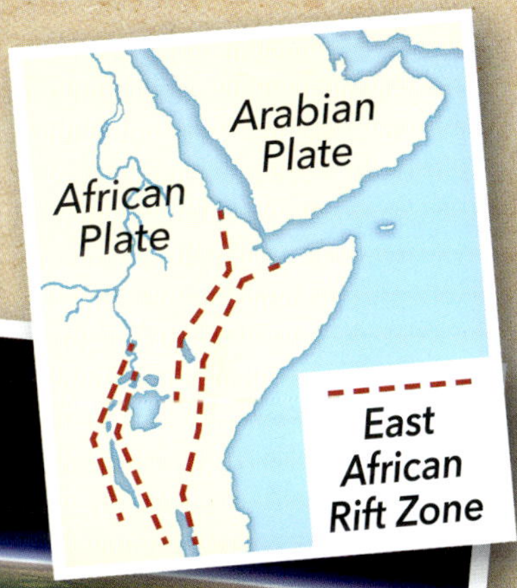

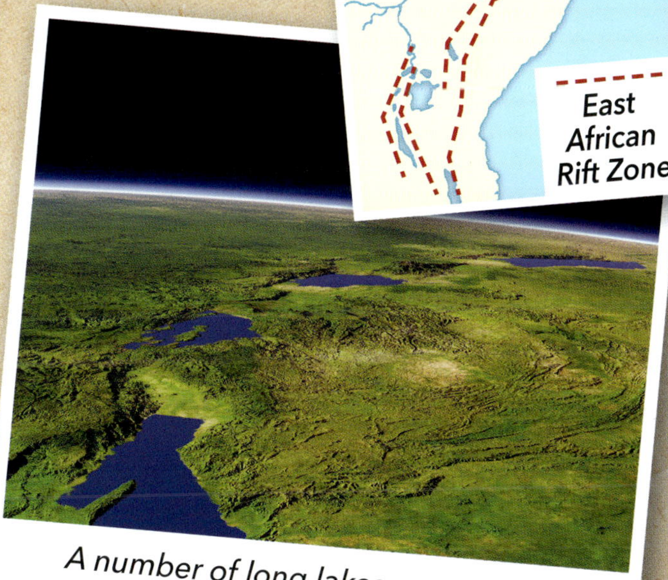

A number of long lakes occur along the site of the rift, where water fills the depressions caused by the very slow splitting of the Earth's crust

The rift, which is a tear in the crust, produces volcanic and earthquake activity along its length. Mount Kilimanjaro is one of these volcanoes.

Africa's Continental Shelf

Where a continent is bounded by an ocean, the land at the ocean's edge often continues under the water as a continental shelf. This shelf may end abruptly at a point where the underwater rocks drop down to a deep ocean abyss.

During the last Ice Age, which ended about 10,000 years ago, the world's sea levels were lower than they are now. At that time, some of Africa's continental shelves were dry land, making the continent much bigger than it is today.

Gouges in the bedrock caused by glaciers are still visible in the landscape of Southern Africa.

Africa's continental shelf regions are important sources of oil and natural gas. Deepwater drilling provides access to these valuable resources.

Where does a continent end?

None of the Earth's seven continents have a definite border. Nations define the exact borders of their country, but not of the continent on which that country lies.

At an ocean boundary, each country in Africa can claim control over the ocean and the continental shelf for a distance of 200 nautical miles from the shore. Member countries of the United Nations set this distance under the UNCLOS agreement.

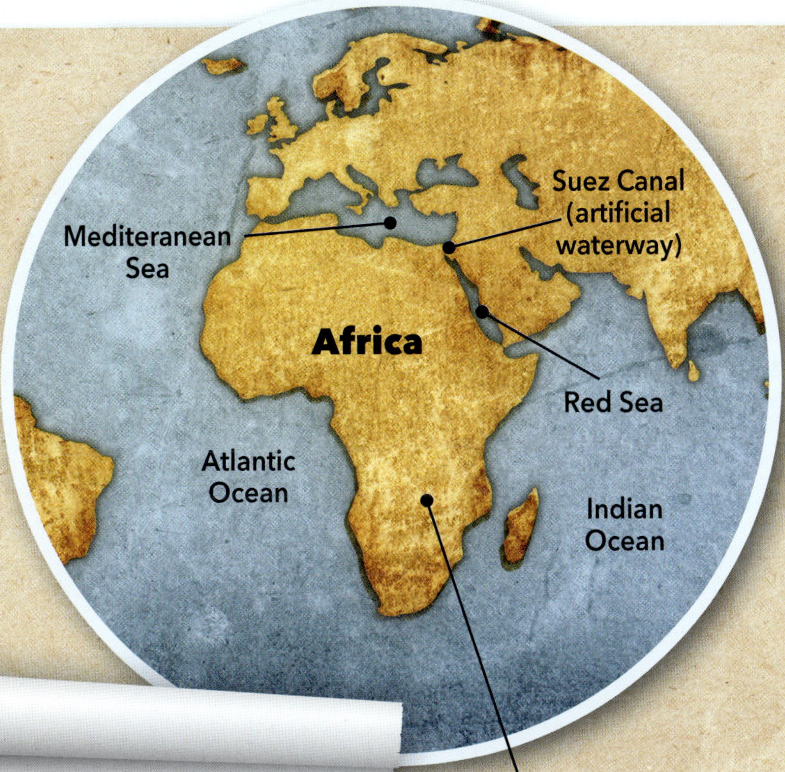

UNCLOS

The United Nations Convention on the Law of the Sea (UNCLOS) sets rules that countries use to determine who has control over the water and the seafloor at a nation's ocean boundary.

Africa is surrounded by water

The Congo Canyon

Beyond the point where the Congo River enters the sea on Africa's west coast, there is a deep canyon under the water. This canyon extends for many kilometres out past the continental shelf and into the Atlantic Ocean.

Unique Heritage

Migration from Africa may have occurred for a variety of reasons including climate change

Birthplace of Humanity

Scientists believe that the ancestors of human beings first evolved in Africa, possibly in the region now called the Horn of Africa. From there, they migrated outwards to all the other places where the first human beings lived.

Ancient Egypt

The culture of the ancient Egyptians still fascinates us. The Egyptian empire lasted for 3,000 years, but people had been living along the banks of the Nile River for as long as 2,000 years before the empire even began.

Ancient Egypt influenced the arts and sciences of many civilisations that came after it.

A version of writing paper derived from the papyrus plant originated in Egypt

The ancient Egyptians improved farming by refining ploughing equipment and utilising irrigation methods

Countries and Cities in Africa

Countries in Africa with the largest populations

There are 54 countries in Africa. The three most populous are Nigeria, Ethiopia and Egypt. The smallest is the island nation of the Seychelles with only about 100,000 people.

Nigeria – over 200 million

Ethiopia – over 110 million

Egypt – over 100 million

Cities

Africa's largest cities are hubs for commerce and higher education. Although more and more people are moving to large cities for work, health services and education, many Africans still have a traditional village lifestyle.

Cape Town, South Africa

Cairo, Egypt

Largest cities in Africa

1. Abidjan, Ivory Coast
2. Alexandria, Egypt
3. Cairo, Egypt
4. Cape Town, South Africa
5. Casablanca, Morocco
6. Kinshasa, Democratic Republic of the Congo
7. Lagos, Nigeria
8. Luanda, Angola
9. Mogadishu, Somalia
10. Nairobi, Kenya

Climate of Africa

Africa has a range of climates

Equatorial Africa

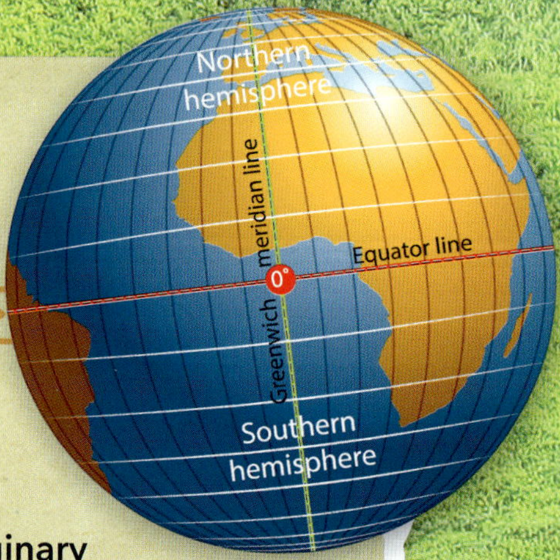

The Equator is the exact halfway mark between the North and South Poles. It is an imaginary line around the surface of the Earth at its widest part, and it passes through the continent of Africa. Countries in this equatorial region have a tropical climate, with high temperatures and high rainfall. The continued existence of Africa's wonderful rainforests depends on this tropical climate.

Zebras and antelopes in Serengeti National Park, Tanzania

Temperate Zones

In the far northwest and far south of the continent, the climate is temperate. This means that the temperatures are mild and there is usually regular rainfall.

Deserts and Grassland Savannahs

To the north and south, away from the Equator, Africa has both deserts and grassland savannahs. In these areas, the lower rainfall is one of the main reasons for the existence of both the Sahara Desert and the grasslands where the lions, giraffes and zebras live.

Africa's Economy

Mining

Africa's export earnings heavily depend on its wealth of raw materials, which include diamonds, gold, natural gas and oil.

Tourism

Tourism is a growing industry in African countries. Wild animal safaris and visits to Africa's natural wonders are high on the list of experiences for international tourists.

Agriculture

Agriculture occupies a large proportion of the workforce in Africa. Egypt and Nigeria are the largest producers of food for the rest of the continent.

Subsistence Farming

Subsistence farming is common throughout Africa's rural areas, where people produce only enough agricultural produce for their own use.

Africa's People

Living on a particular continent is one of the many ways that people define themselves. When people in Africa call themselves Africans, they mean that they have a history that is connected to the African place where they live, or that their ancestors came from.

Culture

There is a rich variety of cultures throughout Africa, each with its own social customs, art forms and mythology.

Population

The population includes many different indigenous peoples, as well as the descendants of mainly European colonists and migrants. The total population of all Africa is about 1.3 billion people, similar to the population in China or India.

Urbanisation

The whole African population is moving from rural to urban areas at a very high rate. By 2050, estimates are that 60% of Africa's people, from all its countries, will be living in cities rather than in rural or natural areas. This mass movement of people to cities is called urbanisation.

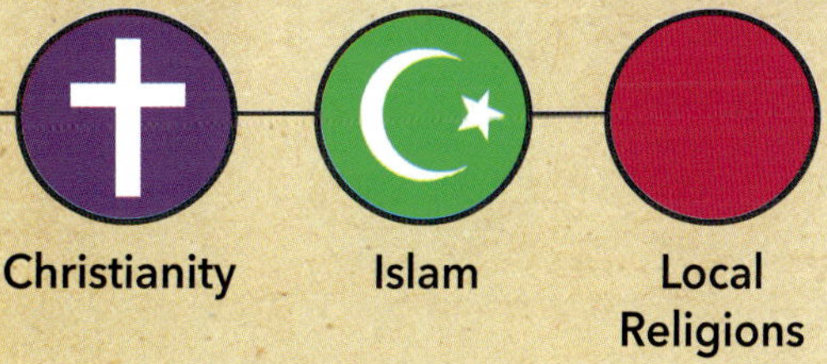

Religion

Africa is home to many local religions, as well as to the introduced religions of Islam, Judaism and Christianity.

The Languages of Africa

There are hundreds of languages spoken throughout the countries of Africa. The most widely used languages are those that have long been useful for trading. These languages include Swahili, Arabic, English and French. Many other languages are spoken within people's own, local communities.

The Environment

Electricity

In many African countries, access to electricity is limited, with about half the supply dependent on the burning of coal and oil. The continent has large reserves of natural gas, which have enormous potential to contribute to Africa's future electricity supply.

Woodfired Methods

Many villagers still burn wood for their cooking and heating needs. This wood is collected from nearby forests and woodlands.

Water Supply

Water is a scarce resource in parts of Africa. Climate change is affecting the savannah areas that border desert regions, threatening to turn them into deserts as well. Hotter temperatures and droughts impact on cities as well as farmers in their fields, affecting people in Africa as in the rest of the world.

Climate Change

Africa is not a large producer of greenhouse gases, despite its population being similar to that of India or China. This is a result of the low level of industrialisation and urbanisation. With increasing development, this situation is likely to change.

Clearing the Land

In the developing regions of southern and central Africa, the clearing of rainforests and reduction of grasslands have become necessary to provide land for the growth in human population. When populations expand, people need to clear more land so that they have room for housing and towns, as well as agricultural land to produce their food.

Places in Africa

❶ Victoria Falls

Victoria Falls is the largest waterfall in Africa, and during the wet season it is the largest waterfall in the world. Located on the Zambezi River, on the border between Zambia and Zimbabwe, Victoria Falls is home to many unique animals and plants, and is one of the most outstanding places in the world.

❷ Table Mountain

Table Mountain is in Cape Town, South Africa. It is near the southern tip of the African continent.

③ Mount Kilimanjaro

The highest mountain in Africa is Mount Kilimanjaro in Tanzania. This dormant volcano is surrounded by rainforest, but is so high that it has glaciers and an ice-covered cap.

④ Lake Victoria

Lake Victoria is the largest lake in Africa and the second largest freshwater lake in the world. Its waters empty into the Nile River.

❺ Atlas Mountains

The Atlas mountain range is in the far northwest of Africa. The mountains separate the Sahara Desert from the Mediterranean and Atlantic coastlines.

❻ Sahara Desert

The Sahara Desert stretches right across northern Africa. It is the largest, sandy desert in the world.

7 Pyramids of Giza

The three Pyramids of Giza are located in Cairo, Egypt. They were built as tombs for Pharaohs and are over 4,500 years old.

8 Timbuktu

Timbuktu is a city in the African nation of Mali. It has an ancient history and was a centre for the study of mathematics and astronomy. The mud-brick buildings of Timbuktu include a large mosque dating from the 1300s.

❾ Nile River

The longest river in the world is the Nile River. It flows for over 6,000 kilometres across Africa before emptying into the Mediterranean Sea. The Nile River was the source of water that allowed ancient Egyptian civilisations to flourish, and it is still vital for agriculture and transport.

Aswan High Dam

The twin temples of Abu Simbel

❿ Aswan High Dam

The Aswan High Dam was built to control the flood cycle of the Nile River, which had regularly flooded crops and villages for thousands of years. Completed in 1971, the dam now stores the floodwaters for controlled release during times of drought. Damming the water also provides the hydroelectric power that has revolutionised the Egyptian economy.

Prior to construction, archaeologists realised that ancient sites would be lost to flooding as the dam filled. Many ancient temples and tombs now rest below these waters.

A nine-year mission to relocate the 3,000-year-old twin temples of Abu Simbel began in 1959. They are now on UNESCO's World Heritage List, after being cut from the cliffs piece-by-piece and reassembled sixty metres higher and 200 metres inland.

⑪ Suez Canal

The Suez Canal was created in 1869 to provide a water link for ships travelling between the Mediterranean Sea, the Red Sea and the Indian Ocean. Before the canal was built, ships from Europe had to travel all the way around the Cape of Good Hope to reach Africa's east coast, or to sail on to India and Southeast Asia.

⑫ Red Sea

The Red Sea is a part of the Great Rift Valley system, which includes the East African Rift. As the crust of the Earth is slowly pushed apart by hot magma rising from deep under the Earth's surface, valleys form along the split and become flooded by oceans. The Red Sea Rift will one day separate the African continent from the Asian continent entirely, and the Red Sea will merge with the Mediterranean Sea. This will be millions of years in the future, and certainly not any time soon!

Wildlife in Africa

Africa has a large number of developing countries. Their increasing populations require more land for homes and businesses and this puts a strain on the environment and its wildlife.

Serengeti

The grassy plains of the Serengeti are home to Africa's iconic wildlife. Lions, elephants, giraffes, wildebeest, jackals, zebras and cheetahs are just a few of the creatures that come to mind when people all around the world think of Africa.

These animals are all savannah, or grassland wildlife, and they do not live throughout the whole continent of Africa.

The climate of the Serengeti is subtropical. The temperature is warm throughout the year, with two rainy seasons and a long dry but relatively cool season.

Madagascar giant day gecko

Madagascar

This large island off the east coast of Africa is an independent nation. Millions of years ago, plate tectonics caused it to break away from the African mainland. This movement isolated Madagascar's wildlife, allowing it to evolve with a unique biodiversity.

The lemurs of Madagascar have become famous worldwide. They are the subject of many wildlife documentaries, and have played the leading roles in animated movies about Madagascar.

Congo River Jungles

The world marvels at Africa's dense jungles. However, the growth in human population has led to these jungles being reduced in size and mostly limited to the regions traversed by the Congo River, the second largest river in Africa.

Humans share a remarkable 98% of their DNA with gorillas!

Great Apes

The African jungles, or rainforests, are home to a magnificent array of wildlife, including the remarkable African gorillas. Highly intelligent and living in close family groups, the rainforest gorillas are under threat and are an endangered species.

Glossary

colonist person who moves to a country and imposes their own culture on the people there

continental shelf edges of a continent that extend outwards underwater

DNA genetic material in a cell

Equator imaginary line around the widest part of the Earth

hydroelectric power electricity generated by falling water turning turbines

iconic special and respected

The savannah of Amboseli National Park, Kenya

jungle dense rainforest

magma molten rocks below the Earth's crust

mythology cultural stories about the ancient past

nautical mile measurement of distance over water or when travelling in the air. It equals 1.85 kilometres

ocean abyss very deep part of an ocean

plate tectonics movement of large blocks of land across the Earth

savannah grasslands in hot regions

subsistence farming producing only enough food for one's own needs

supercontinent landmass made up of most or all of the land on Earth

urbanisation process of moving to live in cities instead of in rural areas

African cities are expanding due to urbanisation

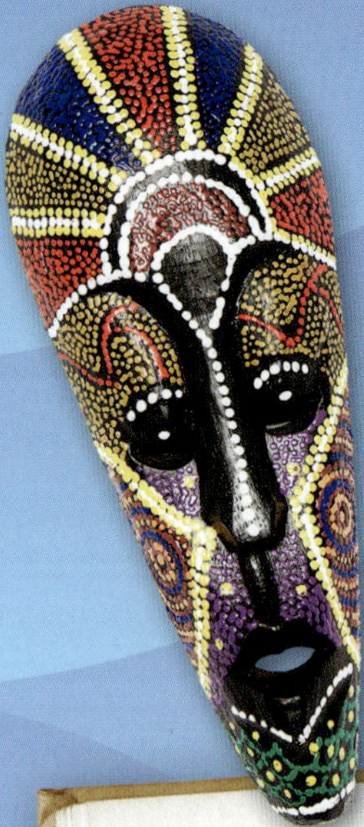

Table Mountain

Index

Victoria Falls, Zimbabwe